JULIAN SCHNABEL

JULIAN SCHNABEL

NEW INDIAN PAINTINGS AND SELECTED SCULPTURE

OCTOBER 16 – NOVEMBER 15

PACEWILDENSTEIN

534 WEST 25TH STREET NEW YORK CITY

UNTITLED (INDIAN 1), 2002, oil and wax on canvas, 7' 6" x 7'

UNTITLED (INDIAN 2), 2002, oil and wax on canvas, 9' x 8'

UNTITLED (INDIAN 3), 2002, oil and wax on canvas, 7' 6" x 7'

UNTITLED (INDIAN 4), 2002, oil and wax on canvas, 9' x 8'

UNTITLED (INDIAN 5), 2002, oil and wax on canvas, 7' 6" x 7'

SMALL HEAD, 1989–90, patinated bronze, 5' 2" x 1' 4" x 1'

JOE, 1987–89, patinated bronze, 12' 2" x 8' 2" x 4'

GRADIVA, 1987–89, patinated bronze, 13' x 5' 7" x 4' 5"

JACQUELINE, 1987, patinated bronze, 8' 8" x 4' 1" x 3' 2"

MYRON, 1985, bronze, 12' x 1' 4" x 1' 4"

YOUNG GIRL IN A BATHTUB, 1987–89, patinated bronze, 3' 6" x 7' 8" x 2' 1"

LEUTWYLER, 1989–90, patinated bronze, 11' 7" x 4' x 4'

Cover: **Untitled (Indian 2)**, 2002 (detail)
Page 5: **Untitled (Indian 3)**, 2002 (detail)
Page 17: **Gradiva**, 1987–89 (detail)

Photography:
Ken Cohen; pages 19 and 31
Bill Jacobson; pages 17, 21, 23, and 29
Phillips/Schwab; page 25
Ellen Page Wilson; cover and pages 5, 7, 9, 11, 13, 15

Design and Production:
Tucker Capparell
Paul Pollard

Color correction:
Motohiko Tokuta

Printing:
Meridian Printing, East Greenwich, Rhode Island, U.S.A.

ISBN: 1-930743-32-7